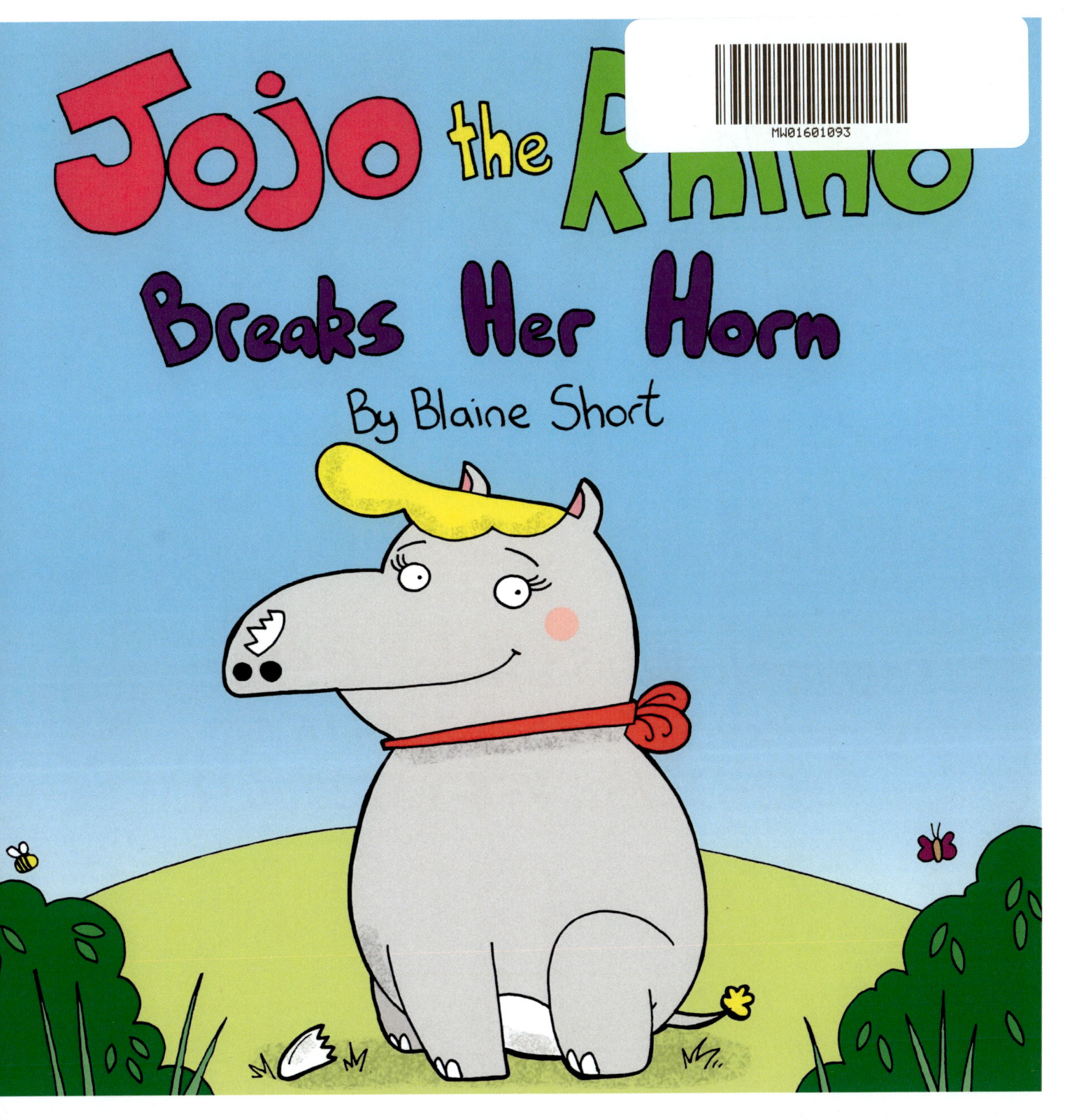

Jojo the Rhino Breaks Her Horn

By Blaine Short

Another night burns away as the sun rises into the savanna sky.

Jojo the rhino yawns and opens her sleepy eyes as she sits up beside her mother.

After breakfast, Jojo decides to take a long walk and see all of her friends.

Jojo the rhino finds Greta the giraffe first. She is scampering in an open field.

"Good morning Jojo," Greta says.

"Good morning Greta," Jojo replies. She runs toward Greta with her horn down.

Greta the giraffe gets scared and runs back to her mother. Jojo the rhino slides to a stop as three lion cubs bounce off of her side.

"I'm sorry Greta!" Jojo shouts, but Greta the giraffe is too far away and doesn't hear her. As the lion cubs scamper off Jojo goes to find another friend.

Next Jojo the Rhino finds Max and Megan the macaws sitting in their home tree.
"Hello Jojo!" squawk the macaws.
"Hello Max! Hello Megan!" Jojo exclaims.

Then Jojo the rhino backs up and slams her horn into their tree and it shakes so hard that Max and Megan the macaws have to fly off. As they fly off two jaguar cubs land on the macaws branch.

"I'm sorry Max! I'm sorry Megan!" Jojo the rhino shouts, but they are too far away and don't hear her. Jojo snorts at the jaguar cubs and trots off to find another friend.

Jojo the rhino finds Biv, Bev, and Buck, the trio of bats, but they are fast asleep. Jojo the Rhino turns to leave. Just then she sees a snake slither toward the sleeping trio of bats. Jojo the rhino bellows and snorts and Biv, Bev, and Buck all wake up and fly away. The snake harmlessly strikes out and hisses.

"I'm sorry Biv! I'm sorry Bev! I'm sorry Buck!" Jojo the rhino yells, but they are too far away and don't hear her. Feeling sad for scaring all her friends, Jojo decides to head home.

Halfway home Jojo the rhino is stopped by the mean warthog. "You're not going this way!" bellows the mean warthog

Jojo the rhino slowly turns around to leave but she finds the three lion cubs have closed in on her. "You're not going this way either," the lion cubs growl.

Quickly Jojo turns to her left getting a little scared. There she finds the two jaguar cubs have blocked her path. "You're not going to go this way or that," the two jaguar cubs tease.

Jojo is very scared now and turns around to find the snake has closed a circle around her. "You're not going anywhere," the snake hisses.

Jojo the rhino, strong and brave, turns to the mean warthog and bellows. She snorts and stomps her feet then she charges the warthog.

The warthog is ready and with his big tusks slams Jojo to the ground. Jojo hears a loud crack as her horn is broken. Jojo the rhino cries softly.

"Silly rhino, you're all alone and just a kid. No one is scared of you here." The mean warthog says. Jojo hides her head.

There is a loud scuffle of hooves and beats of wings. As Jojo listens there are crashes, bangs, and squeals. Jojo the rhino looks up to find her friends and all of their parents surrounding her.

"Are you okay Jojo?" Her mother asks.
"Yes, but I thought I scared all my friends away?" Jojo says.

"Well, you did scare us," chirp the bat trio.
"But our parents told us you were just protecting us," the macaws say.
"So when we heard you were in trouble we came on the double because you're our friend,"
Greta the giraffe says.

"Thank you. You are all very good friends." Jojo the rhino says.
"But what about my horn? I probably look funny."
"Your horn will heal," says her mother, "until then it's just a reminder of how brave you are."

Jojo the rhino, Greta the giraffe, Max and Megan the macaws, and the bat trio - Biv, Bev, and Buck - all went off to play. Surrounded by the adults, of course, for they have learned a valuable lesson. Good friends are always there for each other - especially against bullies.

Made in the USA
Middletown, DE
31 October 2025